The Journey Of A Trailblazing Entrepreneur Martha Stewart

Pauline R. Valerie

Table Of Contents

Introduction

In the world of lifestyle, few names resonate as powerfully as Martha Stewart. She is not just a household name; she is a symbol of reinvention, resilience, and the art of living well.

From humble beginnings in New Jersey to building a media empire that touches the lives of millions, Martha Stewart's journey is nothing short of extraordinary. Her story is a masterclass in turning passion into business, failure into opportunity, and vision into reality. Martha's influence is woven into the fabric of modern consumer culture.

She's the reason we think about table settings with a touch of elegance, why so many people turn to cookbooks for not just recipes but inspiration, and why home décor has become an expression of personal creativity.

But beyond the glamorous image, Martha's life is marked by moments of vulnerability, grit, and, above all, determination. Her rise to success wasn't a straight path, and the obstacles she faced—both personal and professional—only fueled her drive to achieve more. In this biography, we'll delve into the complexities of Martha Stewart's life—the moments of brilliance, the missteps, and the incredible comebacks that define her legacy.

We'll explore how she built an empire from scratch, turned setbacks into opportunities, and ultimately became the first self-made female billionaire in the United States. But beyond her business ventures, we'll also uncover the human side of Martha—the relationships, the challenges, and the personal growth that shaped the woman she is today.

This is not just the story of a woman who redefined the lifestyle industry. It's the story of someone who dared to dream bigger than most, who wasn't afraid to take risks, and who embraced failure as a stepping stone rather than a setback. It's a story that proves success is not just about wealth or fame but about staying true to yourself, adapting to change, and finding joy in the small things.

So, as you turn these pages, prepare to step into the world of Martha Stewart—a world of creativity, entrepreneurship, and, most importantly, resilience. Her story will not only inspire you to think differently about success but also to live your life with intention, elegance, and purpose.

Chapter One; Early Life and Education

Martha Stewart's story begins on August 3, 1941, in Jersey City, New Jersey. She grew up in the suburban town of Nutley, New Jersey, as the second of six children in a hardworking Polish-American family.

Her upbringing was shaped by a blend of discipline, ambition, and creativity—qualities she would later channel into her empire. Her father worked as a pharmaceutical salesman, while her mother juggled roles as a teacher and homemaker. From an early age, Martha displayed a remarkable drive and a natural knack for making the ordinary extraordinary, a talent she undoubtedly inherited from her resourceful mother.

Her family's modest means and strong work ethic instilled in her a sense of determination that would guide her throughout her life. As a teenager, Martha ventured into the world of modeling, a pursuit that came to her quite naturally.

At just 13 years old, she was already posing for fashion shoots and commercials, gracing the pages of magazines and earning her own money. Modeling wasn't just a glamorous escape; it became a practical way to support herself and her ambitions. This early exposure to the spotlight gave her a taste of the poise and confidence she would later carry into her career. Martha's academic journey was equally impressive.

After excelling in high school, she set her sights on Barnard College in New York City, a prestigious institution known for fostering ambitious young women. At Barnard, she initially pursued a major in chemistry but later switched to European and architectural history, fields that aligned with her growing appreciation for art and design.

Her college years were a period of exploration and growth, where she honed her intellectual curiosity and developed a deep appreciation for aesthetics and culture. To fund her studies, Martha continued modeling while attending college, effortlessly balancing her academic pursuits with her professional commitments. Her discipline and time management skills were unmatched, even at a young age.

This dual focus allowed her to graduate in 1962 with a degree that reflected her varied interests and a clear sense of purpose. During her time at Barnard, she also made a personal connection that would shape the next chapter of her life. In 1961, she married Andrew Stewart, a Yale Law School student.

Their union marked the beginning of a partnership that would introduce her to new social and professional circles, laying the groundwork for her future ventures. Martha Stewart's early life is a portrait of ambition, resourcefulness, and a relentless pursuit of excellence. From her humble beginnings in New Jersey to her days as a college student in New York City, she consistently found ways to thrive, setting the stage for the remarkable journey that lay ahead.

Her ability to blend practicality with elegance, even in her formative years, foreshadowed the empire she would one day create.

Chapter Two; Personal Life and Relationship

Martha Stewart's personal life, much like her professional journey, has been filled with triumphs, challenges, and moments of reinvention. She married Andrew Stewart in 1961 while she was still a college student at Barnard.

Together, they built a life that seemed picture-perfect on the surface, including the birth of their daughter, Alexis, in 1965. However, as the years went on, the demands of their individual careers and personal differences began to strain their relationship. Their marriage faced significant challenges, including reported infidelity, which ultimately led to their separation in 1987. By 1990, they finalized their divorce, officially ending nearly three decades of partnership.

Despite this chapter's difficulties, Martha channeled her energy into her growing empire, transforming adversity into fuel for her ambitions. Following her divorce, Martha explored new relationships, including a long-term romance with billionaire Charles Simonyi, a pioneering software engineer known for his work at Microsoft.

Their relationship, though it eventually ended, highlighted Martha's ability to maintain strong connections with people who shared her drive and vision. Beyond her relationships, Martha's love for animals has been a defining aspect of her personal life. She has always been an avid animal lover, surrounding herself with a variety of pets, from dogs and cats to more exotic companions like peacocks. Her homes often reflect this passion, with her properties designed to accommodate her furry and feathered friends.

Speaking of homes, Martha's residences are as much a part of her identity as her recipes and lifestyle tips. She resides in Katonah, New York, where her farmhouse is a serene retreat filled with charm and character. The property reflects her impeccable taste, blending rustic warmth with refined elegance.

In addition to her Katonah estate, she owns a summer home in Maine, a place that serves as both a personal sanctuary and a showcase of her love for design and entertainment. However, not all chapters of Martha's life have been idyllic. In 2004, she faced a major legal challenge when she was convicted of charges related to insider trading. Her trial and subsequent five-month prison sentence became one of the most publicized moments of her career.

Yet, true to form, Martha used this experience as an opportunity for reinvention. She emerged from the ordeal more determined than ever, rebuilding her brand and demonstrating an extraordinary ability to turn setbacks into comebacks.

Martha Stewart's personal journey is a testament to resilience and adaptability. From the joys of motherhood and meaningful relationships to the trials of divorce and legal battles, she has navigated life's complexities with a sense of purpose and an unwavering commitment to her passions. Her story reminds us that even the most successful lives are marked by challenges—and it is how we respond to those challenges that defines our legacy.

Chapter Three; Career

Martha Stewart's career is a story of reinvention, bold choices, and an unparalleled drive to succeed. Her journey began at the tender age of 15 when she stepped into the world of modeling.

With her striking looks and natural poise, she quickly became a sought-after face, gracing magazine covers and earning a steady income. While modeling gave her an early taste of success, it was only the first chapter of her remarkable career. After graduating from Barnard College, Martha took a surprising detour into finance, becoming a stockbroker on Wall Street during the late 1960s and early 1970s.

This role gave her valuable insights into business and investment, skills that would prove essential later in her entrepreneurial ventures. However, the corporate world wasn't her ultimate calling. She left the high-stakes environment of Wall Street to pursue her passion for cooking, entertaining, and creating beautiful spaces.

In 1976, Martha co-founded a small catering business in Westport, Connecticut. What started as a modest venture quickly gained a reputation for its exquisite food, elegant presentations, and impeccable service. Her attention to detail and flair for creating memorable experiences caught the eye of influential clients, and the business flourished. This success led to her first cookbook, Entertaining, published in 1982.

The book was an instant hit, showcasing her innovative ideas and inspiring countless readers to elevate their own hosting skills. It became a bestseller and firmly established Martha as a trusted authority in the domestic arts.

Building on this momentum, Martha continued to expand her influence. She authored more cookbooks, launched a magazine, and became a regular presence on television. In 1996, she took her brand to new heights by founding Martha Stewart Living Omnimedia. This multimedia powerhouse encompassed magazines, television programs, books, and a wide range of household products. Her television show, Martha Stewart Living, became a staple for viewers seeking advice on cooking, decorating, and entertaining.

Under her leadership, the company became synonymous with sophistication and creativity. However, Martha's career wasn't without its challenges. In 2004, she faced a major setback when she was convicted of insider trading, a legal ordeal that led to a five-month prison sentence.

For many, this might have marked the end of their public career, but not for Martha. Demonstrating remarkable resilience, she turned this low point into a new chapter of growth. After her release, she made a triumphant comeback, launching new products, returning to television, and even starring in reality shows. Her ability to bounce back not only solidified her reputation as a businesswoman but also endeared her to a broader audience who admired her determination.

In recent years, Martha has continued to innovate and surprise. She has embraced modern trends, from social media to unique brand collaborations. At 81, she made headlines once again by returning to her modeling roots, gracing the cover of Sports Illustrated's Swimsuit Issue.

Her appearance on the iconic cover was celebrated as a bold statement about aging with confidence and breaking stereotypes. Today, Martha Stewart remains a cultural icon whose influence spans generations. Her media empire continues to thrive, inspiring people to embrace creativity and beauty in their everyday lives. From her early days as a teenage model to her status as a household name, Martha's journey is a testament to perseverance, adaptability, and an unrelenting passion for excellence.

Chapter Four; Health Issues

Martha Stewart, known for her boundless energy and tireless work ethic, has faced her share of health challenges in recent years. In July 2021, she experienced a significant setback when she ruptured her Achilles tendon.

The injury required surgery and a prolonged recovery process that left her temporarily reliant on crutches. For someone as active and independent as Martha, this was undoubtedly a frustrating moment. However, in true Martha fashion, she tackled the situation with resilience and determination, focusing on healing and moving forward.

Despite this injury, Martha remains in remarkably good health, especially for someone in her 80s. She has shared that she doesn't have any major health problems and attributes her vitality to her disciplined approach to wellness. Her commitment to staying healthy is a cornerstone of her lifestyle, and she takes it as seriously as any of her business ventures.

Exercise plays a big role in Martha's routine, and she credits practices like Pilates and horseback riding for keeping her body strong and flexible. These activities not only help her maintain her physical health but also provide her with a sense of joy and connection to the natural world. Horseback riding, in particular, reflects her deep love for animals and the outdoors, a passion that has been part of her life since childhood.

Nutrition is another key pillar of Martha's approach to health. Known for her expertise in cooking and entertaining, she applies the same attention to detail to her own meals. Her diet is rich in fresh, wholesome foods—often sourced directly from her gardens.

From seasonal vegetables to homegrown herbs, her meals are a testament to her belief in the power of good food to nurture both the body and the soul. Now at 82, Martha embraces her age with the same confidence and grace she's displayed throughout her life. She emphasizes the importance of living fully and staying engaged, no matter the number of candles on the birthday cake.

Her mindset is one of curiosity and enthusiasm, whether she's trying something new, working on her business ventures, or spending time with her loved ones. For Martha, every day is an opportunity to create, connect, and thrive.

Her journey through this phase of life serves as an inspiration to many. She's proof that aging doesn't have to mean slowing down or giving up on the things you love. Instead, it can be a time to explore, adapt, and find new ways to enjoy life. By staying active, eating well, and maintaining a positive outlook, Martha continues to set a shining example of how to age with strength, style, and grace.

Even in the face of challenges like her Achilles injury, Martha's resilience and determination remind us that setbacks are temporary and that it's how we respond to them that truly matters. She inspires us not just through her accomplishments but also through her unwavering commitment to living life to its fullest, no matter what comes her way.

Chapter Five; Controversies and Challenges

Martha Stewart's career took a dramatic turn in the early 2000s when she became embroiled in one of the most high-profile insider trading scandals of the decade. In December 2001, she sold shares of ImClone Systems, a pharmaceutical company, just before the stock's value plummeted.

The sale was based on nonpublic information provided by her broker, Peter Bacanovic. By acting on this tip, she avoided a loss of approximately $45,000—a decision that would have lasting consequences. In 2003, the situation escalated when Martha was indicted on multiple charges, including obstruction of justice, conspiracy, and making false statements to federal investigators.

The media frenzy surrounding the case was immense, transforming her from a beloved lifestyle mogul into a lightning rod for public debate about corporate ethics and justice. Her name, once synonymous with elegance and success, was now entangled in legal and moral controversy.

In March 2004, Martha was convicted on four counts related to the investigation. The verdict led to a five-month sentence in a federal prison, followed by two years of supervised release, which included five months of home confinement. For someone who had built an empire on perfection and control, the conviction and its aftermath were humbling, if not devastating.

Yet, in true Martha fashion, she approached the situation with resilience and resolve. Martha served her time at the Federal Prison Camp in Alderson, West Virginia, a minimum-security facility often referred to as "Camp Cupcake" by the media.

During her incarceration, she maintained her composure, reportedly spending her days exercising, gardening, and teaching her fellow inmates skills in crafts and cooking. Her ability to adapt and find purpose even in such challenging circumstances spoke to her resourcefulness and strength of character. When she was released in March 2005, many speculated that her career might be over.

But Martha proved her critics wrong, embarking on one of the most remarkable comebacks in business history. Within months, she was back in the spotlight, launching new products, revamping her television shows, and introducing fresh ventures that breathed new life into her brand.

She turned her legal troubles into a narrative of redemption, one that resonated with audiences who admired her determination and ability to rise above adversity. Martha's post-prison success wasn't just a return to business as usual—it was a reinvention. She embraced the challenges she faced, using them as fuel to rebuild her empire. From launching new television projects to securing lucrative brand partnerships, she demonstrated a level of resilience that solidified her status as a cultural icon.

Her story became a testament to the idea that setbacks, no matter how public or severe, don't have to define one's legacy. Today, Martha Stewart remains a symbol of reinvention and perseverance.

The insider trading scandal, while a significant chapter in her life, is just one piece of a larger story—a story of a woman who refused to let a single misstep overshadow decades of hard work, creativity, and success. Through sheer willpower and unrelenting focus, she reclaimed her place as one of the most influential figures in lifestyle and business, proving that even the most challenging moments can pave the way for new opportunities.

Chapter Six; Achievement, Honor and Award

Martha Stewart's career is a testament to her incredible influence in the lifestyle industry, and her many accolades underscore her enduring impact.

Over the years, her ability to innovate, inspire, and set new standards in cooking, home décor, and entrepreneurship has earned her widespread recognition. These honors are not just awards—they are milestones that highlight the depth of her contributions to her field. One of the most notable aspects of Martha's career is her success in daytime television.

She has won an impressive 12 Daytime Emmy Awards out of 23 nominations, a feat that speaks to her talent as a host and creator. In 2011, she took home the award for Outstanding Lifestyle/Culinary Host, a well-deserved acknowledgment of her ability to connect with audiences through her approachable and elegant style.

Even in 2023, decades into her career, she remained a contender, earning a nomination for Outstanding Daytime Program Host—a reflection of her continued relevance and excellence. Martha's expertise in the culinary world has also been celebrated with prestigious honors like the James Beard Award, which she received in 2014 for her acclaimed television program, Martha Stewart's Cooking School.

This award is one of the highest distinctions in the food industry and solidifies her reputation as a trusted authority in all things culinary. Her ability to teach and inspire through her work has made her a beloved figure for both seasoned cooks and beginners alike.

Her achievements extend beyond television and food. In 1995, Martha was presented with the Golden Plate Award by the American Academy of Achievement, a recognition given to individuals who have reached the pinnacle of their respective fields. Just two years later, in 1997, she was honored with the Edison Achievement Award for her innovative contributions to lifestyle media and product development.

This accolade highlights her role as a trailblazer who transformed the way people think about home and entertainment. Martha's legacy has also been cemented through her induction into various halls of fame.

In 2018, she was inducted into the New Jersey Hall of Fame, an honor that celebrates her roots and her extraordinary success as a native of the Garden State. Two years later, in 2020, she was inducted into the Licensing International Hall of Fame, recognizing her unparalleled ability to build a brand that resonates across industries and generations. These honors serve as a testament to her entrepreneurial spirit and her impact on the global marketplace.

Each of these awards reflects a different facet of Martha Stewart's career—her creativity, business acumen, and ability to connect with audiences. But more than that, they tell the story of a woman who has redefined what it means to be a lifestyle expert.

From hosting award-winning television shows to authoring best-selling books and developing successful product lines, Martha has continually set the bar higher. These accolades aren't just markers of her past achievements—they are a reminder of the legacy she continues to build. Martha's story is one of perseverance, innovation, and a relentless pursuit of excellence. Her ability to evolve with the times while staying true to her vision has made her an icon, not just in the lifestyle industry but in the broader world of business and culture.

Whether she's accepting an Emmy or a James Beard Award, each honor underscores the enduring influence of Martha Stewart's work.

Chapter Seven: Net Worth

Martha Stewart's journey to wealth is as remarkable as her career itself. As of 2024, her net worth is estimated to be around $400 million, a testament to her resilience and ability to adapt in the ever-changing business landscape.

Her financial success has been built on a foundation of creativity, hard work, and an unrelenting drive to stay ahead of the curve. In 2000, Martha achieved a milestone few could dream of—becoming a billionaire. This landmark moment came when her company, Martha Stewart Living Omnimedia, went public, marking the first time a woman had become a self-made billionaire in the United States through a company she founded.

The IPO was a massive success, catapulting her brand and her personal wealth to unprecedented heights. Her empire included magazines, cookbooks, television shows, and a vast array of products, making her a household name synonymous with elegance and domestic expertise.

However, her meteoric rise hit a significant hurdle in 2004. Following her conviction in an insider trading scandal, Martha faced not only legal consequences but also a sharp decline in her company's stock value. The fallout from the controversy caused her net worth to plummet, and many speculated whether she could recover from such a public and financial setback.

True to her indomitable spirit, Martha didn't allow this challenge to define her. Instead, she focused on rebuilding, demonstrating the same entrepreneurial grit that had driven her success in the first place. Over the years, she diversified her ventures, creating new revenue streams that helped her regain her financial footing.

Cookbooks, which had always been a cornerstone of her brand, continued to sell well, thanks to their timeless appeal and practical value. Her television presence remained strong, with new shows and collaborations that kept her in the public eye. Branding deals also played a crucial role in Martha's comeback. She partnered with major retailers and launched products that resonated with her audience, from home goods to kitchenware.

These ventures not only generated significant income but also reinforced her reputation as a tastemaker and innovator. Her ability to understand her audience's desires and deliver high-quality products has been a consistent factor in her financial success.

What makes Martha's financial story so compelling is not just the numbers but the narrative of reinvention. She turned what could have been a career-ending scandal into an opportunity to start anew, proving that setbacks, even on a grand scale, can be overcome with determination and vision. Her ability to navigate these challenges has made her a role model for entrepreneurs and creatives alike.

Today, Martha Stewart's $400 million net worth reflects more than just monetary value—it represents decades of influence, innovation, and resilience.

Her journey offers a powerful reminder that wealth is not just about financial gain but about creating something enduring, adapting to challenges, and finding new ways to thrive. Through it all, she remains a pioneer in the lifestyle industry, inspiring millions to live beautifully and purposefully.

Chapter Eight; Facts About Her

Martha Stewart's life took a dramatic and unexpected turn in 2004 when she became embroiled in a high-profile legal battle that captured the nation's attention. The incident stemmed from an insider trading scandal involving ImClone Systems, a pharmaceutical company.

While Martha was not convicted of insider trading itself, she faced charges of obstruction of justice and making false statements during the investigation. The outcome was a conviction that led to her serving five months in federal prison—a striking fall from grace for the lifestyle icon who had built an empire around perfection and success.

The trial and subsequent prison sentence became a defining moment in Martha's life and career. The media frenzy surrounding her case was relentless, with every detail scrutinized and debated.

For someone who had meticulously crafted a public image of elegance and control, the experience was undoubtedly humbling. Yet, even during this challenging period, Martha displayed the resilience and tenacity that had always been at the core of her success. In October 2004, Martha reported to the Federal Prison Camp in Alderson, West Virginia, often referred to as "Camp Cupcake" in the press. Despite the nickname, the experience was no vacation.

However, Martha made the most of her time there, reportedly forming bonds with fellow inmates and contributing by teaching classes in cooking and crafting. Her ability to adapt to such an unfamiliar and challenging environment spoke volumes about her character.

The conviction and prison time marked a turning point in her career, but rather than letting it define her, Martha used it as an opportunity to reinvent herself. Upon her release in March 2005, many doubted whether she could recover from such a public and personal setback. But Martha proved them wrong. With remarkable determination, she set about rebuilding her brand, showing the world that resilience and reinvention were just as much a part of her story as success and creativity.

Her comeback began almost immediately. Martha returned to the public eye with a renewed focus and energy, launching new television shows and expanding her product lines.

She leaned into the narrative of redemption, allowing her audience to see her not just as a perfectionist but as a human being who had faced challenges and emerged stronger. This relatability endeared her to a wider audience and gave her brand a fresh perspective. Financially, Martha Stewart Living Omnimedia, the company she founded, rebounded from the hit it had taken during the scandal. New ventures and collaborations breathed life back into the brand, and within a few years, it was once again thriving.

Martha's ability to turn adversity into opportunity became an integral part of her legacy, inspiring entrepreneurs and fans alike. What makes this chapter of Martha Stewart's life so compelling is the way she confronted adversity head-on. She didn't shy away from her mistakes or try to rewrite the past.

Instead, she acknowledged her challenges and used them as a springboard to evolve both personally and professionally. Her story is a powerful reminder that setbacks, no matter how public or painful, can be overcome with resilience, hard work, and a willingness to adapt. Today, Martha Stewart's name is once again synonymous with success. While the insider trading scandal remains a part of her story, it is far from the whole story.

It serves as a reminder of her humanity and her ability to rise above even the most difficult circumstances. For Martha, the experience was not the end of her journey but rather a new beginning—one that allowed her to reimagine her legacy and continue to inspire millions around the world.

Chapter Nine; Legacy

Martha Stewart's legacy stands as a testament to innovation, resilience, and vision, as she is widely regarded as the pioneer of the modern lifestyle brand.

Long before the term "influencer" became part of the cultural lexicon, Martha was revolutionizing the way people approached cooking, home décor, and everyday living. She not only introduced the world to her unique blend of elegance and practicality but also built an empire that forever changed consumer culture.

Her groundbreaking moment came in 1999 when Martha Stewart Living Omnimedia went public. This move made her the first self-made female billionaire in the United States—a monumental achievement that cemented her place in history.

It wasn't just a financial milestone; it was a cultural one. Martha redefined the possibilities for women entrepreneurs, proving that creative vision and business acumen could coexist on an extraordinary scale. At the heart of Martha's influence is her uncanny ability to connect with her audience. Her brand isn't just about products or shows; it's about a way of life—one that emphasizes beauty, quality, and intentional living.

Whether it's a perfectly roasted Thanksgiving turkey, a beautifully organized garden, or a flawlessly set table, Martha has inspired millions to elevate the everyday. Her reach is staggering, with her brand engaging approximately 100 million consumers every month.

From magazines to television, cookbooks to product lines, her presence spans countless platforms, showcasing her mastery of multimedia and her deep understanding of what her audience craves. But Martha's impact goes far beyond aesthetics. She has played a pivotal role in shaping modern consumer behavior, particularly in the lifestyle sector. Long before social media influencers began promoting curated living, Martha was setting the standard, blending expertise with accessibility.

Her work has empowered people to see their homes, meals, and celebrations as canvases for creativity and expression. Martha's career hasn't been without challenges. The legal troubles she faced in the early 2000s, including her prison sentence, could have derailed her legacy.

Yet, her response to adversity became one of the most compelling aspects of her story. Rather than allowing setbacks to define her, Martha used them as opportunities for reinvention. She emerged from those challenges stronger, proving that resilience and adaptability are just as important as innovation in the journey of entrepreneurship.

This ability to thrive in the face of adversity is a key reason Martha remains an enduring icon. She has not only rebuilt her brand but expanded it in new and exciting directions. Collaborations, fresh product lines, and even her return to modeling at the age of 81 have demonstrated that her creative spirit is as vibrant as ever.

Martha's journey serves as a reminder that reinvention is always possible, no matter the stage of life or career. Her influence has also inspired a new generation of creators and entrepreneurs. Many of today's lifestyle influencers and content creators owe a debt to the path she paved. Martha didn't just create a brand; she built a blueprint for others to follow, showing how to turn passion into a thriving business.

Her work has elevated entire industries, from food and home goods to media and retail, leaving a lasting imprint that goes far beyond her own success. Martha Stewart's story is one of vision, determination, and an unwavering commitment to excellence.

From her early days as a caterer to her reign as a media mogul, she has continually redefined what it means to be an entrepreneur. Her legacy is not just about wealth or influence—it's about the millions of people she has inspired to live more beautifully, creatively, and intentionally. In a world that constantly evolves, Martha's ability to adapt while staying true to her core values ensures that her name will remain synonymous with elegance and innovation for generations to come.

Conclusion

As we reach the final pages of this journey through Martha Stewart's extraordinary life, it's clear that her story is far more than a collection of accomplishments and setbacks. It's a testament to resilience, vision, and the power of reinvention.

From her early days in New Jersey to her rise as a self-made billionaire, from facing legal challenges to making a stunning comeback, Martha Stewart has continuously demonstrated that true success is not just about where you begin but about how you navigate the twists and turns along the way.

Her legacy is undeniable. Martha has not only reshaped the way we think about cooking, home décor, and lifestyle, but she has also paved the way for countless entrepreneurs, particularly women, to follow in her footsteps.

Her brand is synonymous with elegance, creativity, and a commitment to excellence, and her influence extends far beyond her television shows, cookbooks, and product lines. In a world of constant change, Martha has remained constant, evolving with the times while never losing sight of the values that made her a household name.

The story of Martha Stewart is one of grit, determination, and an unwavering belief in the power of hard work and innovation. She's proven time and time again that setbacks, no matter how significant, do not define a person's future. Instead, it's how we respond to those challenges that shapes our true legacy.

As you've come to understand, Martha's journey isn't just about success; it's about the human spirit's capacity to overcome, adapt, and thrive. Her story is a reminder that there is always room for reinvention and growth, no matter where we are in life. It's about taking risks, embracing change, and always striving to be the best version of ourselves, both personally and professionally.

Thank you for joining me on this odyssey through the life of one of the most influential figures of our time. I hope that, in reading her story, you've been inspired to pursue your own passions with the same relentless drive that has made Martha Stewart a true icon. Her journey is proof that with determination, creativity, and an open mind, anything is possible.